Everybody Digs Soil

HOW IS SOIL MADE?

Heather L. Montgomery

Crabtree Publishing Company

www.crabtreebooks.com

Crabtree Publishing Company

www.crabtreebooks.com

Author: Heather L. Montgomery
Editor-in-Chief: Lionel Bender
Editor: Lynn Peppas
Project coordinator: Kathy Middleton
Photo research: Susannah Jayes
Designer: Ben White
Production coordinator: Ken Wright
Production: Kim Richardson
Prepress technician: Ken Wright

Consultant: Heather L. Montgomery, children's writer, environmental educator, and science education consultant who runs Dragonfly Programs: http://www.dragonflyeeprograms.com

Cover: In composting, fungi and bacteria help break down organic waste to add nutrients to the soil.

Title page: Preparing the soil for planting

This book was produced for Crabtree Publishing Company by Bender Richardson White.

Photographs and reproductions:
© Getty Images: pages 4/5 (Alistair Berg), 6/7 (Chris Whitehead), 9 (Jim Nigel Cattlin)
© iStockphoto.com: Headline image (redmal), pages 8 (redmal), 10 (Martin Lovatt), 11 top (Oliver Sun Kim), 11 bottom (AVTG), 12 (Victor Prikhodko), 13 top (Denis Pogostin), 13 bottom (Tony Campbell), 14 (Lisa Fletcher), 14/15 (Marcin Pawinski), 15, 16 (lilly3), 16/17 (Charles Braaten), 20/21 (Dave Hughes), 22/23 (David Freund), 23 bottom (Karen Moller), 23 top (JulienGrondin), 26 (PaulRoux), 27 (Sasha Radosavljevic), 28/29 (Ints T omsons), 29 (MaciejBogacz)
© Getty Images/Jupiterimages: cover (boy)
© Science Photo Library: page 7 (Eye Of Science)
© www.shutterstock.com: cover (bottom compost), title page (Rosinka), pages 5 (Bjarne Henning Kvaale), 6 (skeletoriad), 9 bottom (Pakhnyushcha), 17 (Stacy Barnett), 18 (Mark Smith), 19 top (Elena Elisseeva), 19 right (Jim Parkin), 21 (Lee Prince), 24 (David P. Lewis), 25 top (Mariusz S. Jurgielewicz), 25 bottom (HannahEckman), 26/27 (Dr. Morley Read), 27 (Vladimir Chernyanskiy)
USDA Natural Resources Conservation Service: page 4

Library and Archives Canada Cataloguing in Publication

Montgomery, Heather L.
    How is soil made? / Heather L. Montgomery.

(Everybody digs soil)
Includes index.
ISBN 978-0-7787-5401-5 (bound).--ISBN 978-0-7787-5414-5 (pbk.)

    1. Soils--Juvenile literature. 2. Soil ecology--Juvenile literature.
I. Title. II. Series: Everybody digs soil

S591.3.M65 2010   j631.4   C2009-906272-0

Library of Congress Cataloging-in-Publication Data

Montgomery, Heather L.
 How is soil made? / Heather L. Montgomery.
    p. cm. -- (Everybody digs soil)
 Includes index.
 ISBN 978-0-7787-5414-5 (pbk. : alk. paper) -- ISBN 978-0-7787-5401-5
(reinforced library binding : alk. paper)
 1. Soils--Juvenile literature. 2. Soil ecology--Juvenile literature. I. Title.
II. Series: Everybody digs soil.
 S591.3.M66 2009
 631.4--dc22
                                        2009042780

Crabtree Publishing Company

www.crabtreebooks.com   1-800-387-7650

Printed in the U.S.A./122009BG20090930

Published in Canada
Crabtree Publishing
616 Welland Ave.
St. Catharines, Ontario
L2M 5V6

Published in the United States
Crabtree Publishing
PMB 59051
350 Fifth Avenue, 59th Floor
New York, New York 10118

Published in the United Kingdom
Crabtree Publishing
Maritime House
Basin Road North, Hove
BN41 1WR

Published in Australia
Crabtree Publishing
386 Mt. Alexander Rd.
Ascot Vale (Melbourne)
VIC 3032

CONTENTS

WHAT IS SOIL?

Soil is more than just dirt. It is a mixture of living and non-living material. Since the beginning of Earth, soil has been forming. It will continue changing as long as the Sun, wind, water, plants, and animals are around to affect it.

GROWING SOIL

Soil starts life as rock. Any exposed rock is eroded, or worn down, by weather. After many natural processes and thousands of years, worn-down rock, air, water, and **organic** matter form soil. Organic matter is anything that is or has been alive. It includes plant roots, worms, bacteria, plus dead plant and animal pieces.

▲ Planting seeds in the garden

▲ Soil includes dead matter such as turkey droppings and wood chips.

4

YOU DIG IT

Grab some damp soil. Rub it between your fingers. Does it feel gritty? Then it is made of sand. Slippery? It has silt-sized grains. Sticky? It must be clay.

IT TAKES ALL TYPES

Thousands of types of soil cover our planet. Soils differ in type of rocks they are made from, how old they are, and the processes that helped to make them. **Mineral** soil is the part made from rock and gives soil its texture. Sandy soil has large grains of rock in it. **Silty** soil has smaller rock bits—to see them you need a microscope. Clay soil has even tinier pieces. For your garden soil, you want a mixture of rock pieces of all sizes.

SOIL INGREDIENTS

❋ Soil is a mix of:
- 45% rock material
- 25% air
- 25% water
- 5% organic matter

▲ *Broken-up rock is the starting material for many kinds of soil.*

ALL ABOUT HUMUS

Decayed or rotting plant and animal matter is called **humus**. It gives soil that dark, rich color and provides **nutrients**. Without humus, soil is not **fertile**—plants cannot grow in it.

CRUMMY SOIL

Humus is sticky. It clumps with the mineral soil to form crumbs of earth. The crumbs cling to nutrients and then free them slowly as plants need them. Soil without any humus lets nutrients leak away too fast. Humus also holds water and stops soil being washed or blown away by rain and winds.

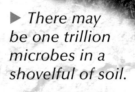

► There may be one trillion microbes in a shovelful of soil.

HIDDEN HEROES

What makes humus? **Decomposers!** Many animals—including vultures, millipedes, worms, dung beetles, and termites—eat dead material. They take in bits of leaves, stems, flowers, and dead bodies and digest them. Their droppings then add to the humus.

◄ Maggots eat dead flesh. Then they return the nutrients to the ground in their droppings.

MICROBES

The decomposition All-Stars are microbes, such as fungi and bacteria. Dead plants are full of energy and nutrients, but these are locked away in organic material that larger creatures cannot break down. Fungi and bacteria work their way in with special chemicals called **enzymes** to tackle the tough jobs.

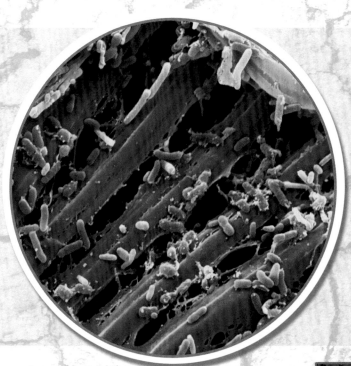

▶ Bacteria are microscopic life forms. They are found in soil, water, air, animals, and plants.

7

NUTRIENTS IN SOIL

Nutrients are the life-supporting parts of soil. A plant uses air and sunlight for energy, but everything else it must get from the ground. To survive, a plant needs 16 different soil nutrients. These come from rocks, organic matter, or fertilizers.

MAJOR PLAYERS

Nitrogen, phosphorus, and potassium are the main soil nutrients needed by plants. Without one of these, a plant cannot perform **photosynthesis**, make leaves, produce fruit, or grow roots. Through photosynthesis, plants use the energy of sunlight to join water and oxygen in air to make their own food materials.

◀ *A young plant grows leaves to get sunlight and roots to get nutrients from soil.*

HOW MUCH?

Crops are the plants farmers grow for food and useful materials. Healthy crops may need from 50 to 150 pounds (23 to 68 kilograms) of the main soil nutrients per acre (the size of a football field). Because of this, these nutrients are often the first ones used up. Nutrients exist in many different forms. Plants can use some of these forms, but not others. Humus crumbs hold nutrients in forms that plants can use. Water **dissolves** nutrients that plants can then suck up.

▼ *This plant does not have enough nitrogen to keep all its leaves green. If it does not get some quick, it will not survive.*

PUMPING IRON

The iron in the red blood cells pumping through your heart was a nutrient from the soil. Originally, the iron was part of a rock. It rusted out of the rock and joined the soil. Then, maybe a potato plant slurped it up. Later, you gobbled some mashed potatoes, and the iron became part of your blood.

PICKY PLANTS

Rainforest trees can be picky eaters. Scientists discovered that certain types of trees would only live where particular nutrients were plentiful.

Healthy sunflower plants—a sign of fertile soil

NUTRIENT CYCLES

All its life, an oak tree sucks nutrition from the soil. When the tree dies, it crashes down. The nutrients are locked away in the wood. A decomposing fungus recycles the nutrients into the humus. Then, a sapling can use the nutrients and slowly grow into a new tree.

BREAKING THE CYCLE

In nature, nutrients get recycled. They just keep going in circles. When humans harvest, or collect, grain, fruits, or vegetables, they take organic matter out of the natural cycle. Fewer nutrients are left for recycling. Soil can run out of nutrients like phosphorus, which **leaches**, or washes, out of the soil and ends up at the bottom of the ocean. Farmers must make sure they balance the nutrients their crops take out of the soil with nutrients added back in through fertilizer.

▼ *A rotting tree will provide nutrients for new plants to grow.*

YOU DIG IT

Put food scraps in a bucket with a handful of soil. Leave the bucket outdoors. Watch the scraps for a month to see decomposition in action.

PLANT PALS

Nitrogen is in the air and soil all around us, but not in a usable form. Lightning can "fix" or change ordinary nitrogen so that plants can use it. Some plants, called **legumes**—beans, peas, and clover—have found another way. Bacterial buddies live on their roots. The bacteria fix nitrogen for the plants, and the plants give the bacteria sugar and a place to live.

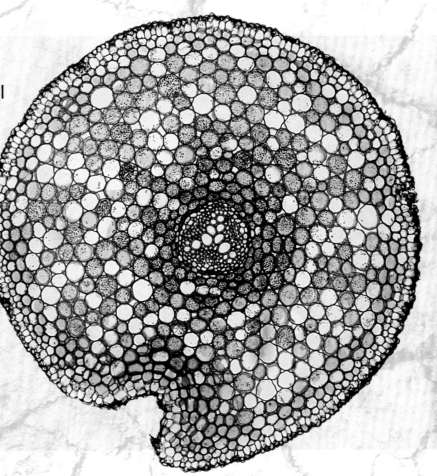

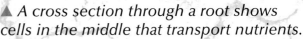
▲ A cross section through a root shows cells in the middle that transport nutrients.

ROOT ZONE

Almost all trees have fungi that live right on their roots and help recycle nutrients. Some microbes even live inside of the root cells! They extend long thread-like parts of their body into the soil to collect nutrients to share with the plant.

◄ The forest floor is covered in decaying leaves that feed the roots of the growing trees.

11

WATER FOR LIFE

All life needs water. The type of soil, its texture, and the amount of humus it has affects how water travels through it. This affects all living things in the soil.

DRINK IT UP!

Water can fill the **pores**, or small spaces, between the crumbs of soil. When a root sucks water out of the pores, the largest ones empty first until there is only a thin film of water clinging to the pieces of soil. At that point, a root cannot get any more to drink.

CRUMMY SPACES

Soil with good structure has crumbs of various sizes allowing the water to move through it. Sandy soil has such large pores that water runs right through it, carrying nutrients away. Pieces of clay soil fit together so tightly that rainwater may never soak in.

▶ *Raindrops fall on the soil's surface then soak in.*

YOU DIG IT

Fill a jar with golf balls or similar-sized balls. Fill an identical jar with marbles or other small balls. Which jar has more pores? Larger pores? Do you think they will hold the same amount of water? Add water to find out.

LIQUID HELP

Water in the soil has another important role. Just like the powder for a drink dissolves in your glass, nutrients dissolve in rainwater and then are available to plants. Too much water can leach the nutrients out of the soil and wash them away.

▶ *Plants need extra help with water when the weather is dry.*

DROWNED GROUND

In a flooded field, water fills all of the space in the soil so there is no room for air. Earthworms, millipedes, and other soil creatures try to climb to the surface before they drown.

▶ *A flooded field after heavy rain*

FRESH AIR

Every living thing needs air. Animals need to get oxygen from the air and get rid of carbon dioxide into air. Plants need to get carbon dioxide from air and get rid of oxygen into it. How does fresh air travel through the soil?

AERATORS

Getting fresh air in and out of soil is known as **aeration**. Animals that tunnel help this to happen. Earthworms are famous aerators, but any digging animal can do the job.

SOIL AIR

Underground air is not the same as what we breathe. Soil creatures use up some of the oxygen, so there is not as much available. The deeper you go in soil, the less oxygen there is.

AERATOR FACTS

✳ Earthworms are probably the greatest aerators of soil because of their great numbers. A square yard (0.9 sq m) of soil can be home to more than 700 earthworms.

✳ Some nematodes— another type of worm— grow to 10 feet (3 m) long. They all start life as tiny creatures. They take a year to become adults.

▶ *A handful of useful worms*

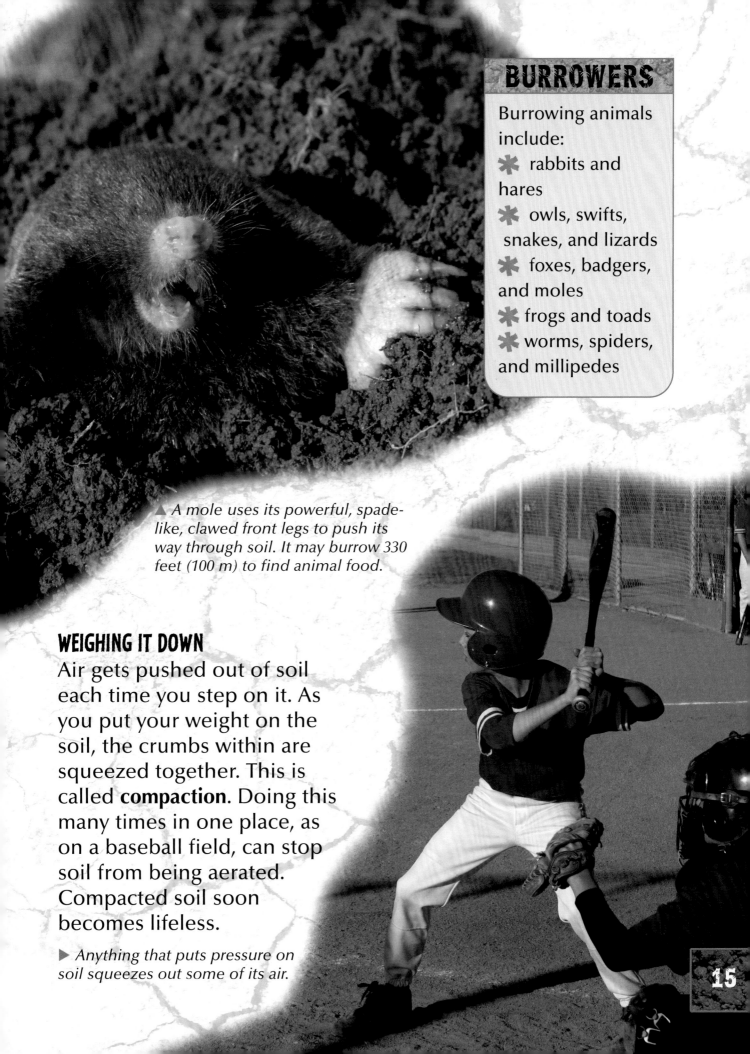

BURROWERS

Burrowing animals include:
* rabbits and hares
* owls, swifts, snakes, and lizards
* foxes, badgers, and moles
* frogs and toads
* worms, spiders, and millipedes

▲ *A mole uses its powerful, spade-like, clawed front legs to push its way through soil. It may burrow 330 feet (100 m) to find animal food.*

WEIGHING IT DOWN

Air gets pushed out of soil each time you step on it. As you put your weight on the soil, the crumbs within are squeezed together. This is called **compaction**. Doing this many times in one place, as on a baseball field, can stop soil from being aerated. Compacted soil soon becomes lifeless.

▶ *Anything that puts pressure on soil squeezes out some of its air.*

WEATHERING ROCK

Soil starts with rock. The rock is broken down through **weathering**, a process that turns boulders to pebbles, and pebbles to bits of mineral and soil particles.

PLANT POWER

Weathering can be done by living things, by physical force, or by chemicals. Plants have rock-splitting power. A root might push its way into a gap in the rock. As the plant takes nutrients from the rock and grows, it pushes the crack wider year-by-year. Gravity, the force that pulls everything down, will finish the job.

ICE WEDGE

Ice can weather rock. When water in a rock freezes, it gets bigger and makes a tiny crack. Over years of freezing and thawing, the rock will split. Salt can act like a wedge, too. Rainwater carries salts into the rock's pores then dries up. The salt crystals will grow and can rupture the rock.

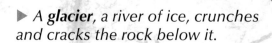
► A **glacier**, a river of ice, crunches and cracks the rock below it.

16

HIT BY GRIT

Wind and water can carry **sediment**—sand and other small pieces of rock. When the sediment is washed or blown against a rock, it chips away at it. After thousands of years, a canyon, cave, or beautiful rock sculpture may be formed.

▼ *A rock face showing layers of different-colored, weathered rock*

◄ *The rocks beside this water are being split apart by plants growing on them.*

BREAK IT DOWN

Rocks can be weathered chemically, too. Their makeup can be changed so that they become softer and fall apart.

ROTTING ROCKS

Water changes the chemical nature of rock. It can rust the iron out of rocks. Much of Earth is made of granite, a very hard rock. Water weathers granite into sand and clay and releases potassium and other nutrients. In time, these materials become part of soil.

ACID RAIN GO AWAY!

Rainwater can be naturally **acidic**. When people add certain chemicals like carbon dioxide to the air, the rainwater becomes acid rain. Acid rain can eat right through rock, wearing away statues, tombstones, and boulders.

▼ *Pollution can mix with the air and create acid rain, which changes the chemistry of soil.*

▲ Stalactites (coming down) are made by the action of water on rocks.

▲ Lichen can live where no other plant has lived before.

COLUMNS OF CALCIUM

Have you noticed columns of minerals in a cool cave? Stalagmites (going up) and stalactites (coming down) are made by the action of water on rocks. As water runs through certain rocks, it dissolves calcium and other minerals. When the water drips into a cave, it leaves the minerals behind.

ROCK REDUCER

A **lichen** is a combination of fungus and alga that live together. It has the power to dissolve rock! The lichen releases chemicals to eat away at the rock. Once the lichen has softened the rock, plants can move into the area. Simple plants, such as mosses and ferns, often appear first after lichen.

CARRIED AWAY

Erosion is when soil or rocks are carried from one place to another. Like weathering, many forces—water, wind, gravity, and people—can cause erosion. Weathering and erosion, working together, have created the landscape of Earth.

MIGHTY MISSISSIPPI

Whether it is a tiny trickle or a raging river, water carries a lot of soil. The Mississippi River moves 500 million tons (450 million metric tons) of sediment every year. Silt and clay particles float downstream, making the water cloudy. Sand and pebbles bounce along the bottom causing more weathering as they go. Together they are carried toward the sea.

▼ *Delicate Arch at Arches National Park, Utah, has been formed by weathering and erosion.*

THE HUMAN HAND

People can cause erosion, too. When plants are removed, the rain pounds the **topsoil**. Each raindrop hits with a force that can move humus and minerals downhill. Although erosion is a natural process, human action sometimes helps it along. Mining, roadbuilding, rock quarries, and construction work all shift tons of rock.

▶ In surface mines, rock is dug out and removed.

21

DUMPED ON THE LAND

After erosion happens, the soil is dumped on land or in the ocean. This is known as deposition. It can destroy yards and houses but can also enrich soil and build new land.

DELTA FORCE

When a river full of sediment reaches its mouth, it slows down. With the help of gravity, the sediment falls out, forming new land, called a delta. The land grows into the sea.

LANDSLIDE!

Mudslides and landslides shift and dump tons of rock and soil. They can fill in valleys, move roads, and cover entire houses. Even though they are destructive, they play an important role in uncovering new rock and minerals to help build new soil.

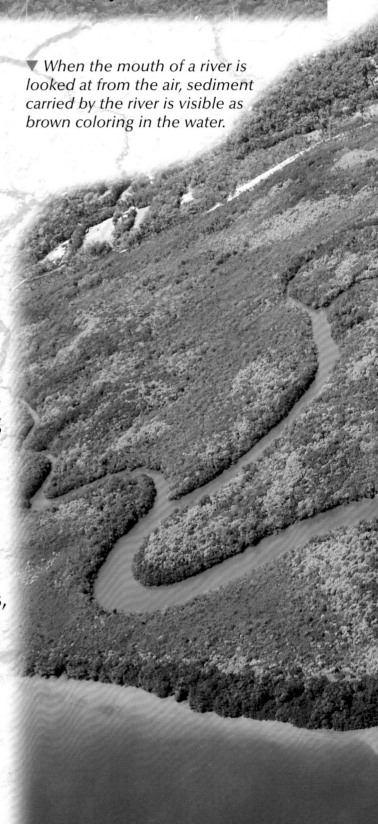

▼ *When the mouth of a river is looked at from the air, sediment carried by the river is visible as brown coloring in the water.*

▲ *A river of red hot lava*

RAINING SOIL

When a volcano erupts, it spews tons of rock bits into the air. It has to fall somewhere. Full of minerals such as iron, it covers the land and adds to the soil.

COVERED UP

During a flood, a river may flow over its banks and spread out over surrounding low land. As the water slows down, it drops its sediment. People who live along the Nile River in Egypt take advantage of this. Each year, sediment full of nutrients is added to their fields as natural fertilizer!

▲ *The banks of the Nile River are rich agricultural land.*

23

SOIL AND CLIMATE

All across Earth, climate makes a difference. Climate is the average weather over a long period. Hot or cold, windy or rainy, the soil feels the climate.

TOO COLD FOR COMFORT

In cold windy areas, like the **tundra**, the wind can easily erode soil. In addition, the usual decomposers, such as bacteria, cannot stand the cold. Dead plant and animal matter just builds up. Few nutrients are recycled into the soil.

DRY DESERTS

With little rain, desert soil is full of sand that never gets broken down. Water drains through sand quickly, making it hard for plants to grow. That means there is very little organic matter added to the soil. Nutrients such as calcium turn the desert soil **basic** (the opposite of acidic) because they are not leached out. Cactus plants like basic soil but most plants do not.

▼ *Joshua trees have deep root systems that help them reach water in deserts.*

SOIL FACTS

✳ Rain forests get so much rain that it washes nutrients right out of the soil. Rainforest soils are some of the most nutrient-starved on the planet.

✳ Rainforest soils are acidic. This prevents the growth of many soil bacteria. This is why rainforest leaf litter breaks down slowly.

SUPER TREES

In areas where there is plenty of water and nutrients, forests can grow. Trees can change the soil. Trees provide organic matter to be recycled, keeping the soil fertile. Their roots hold the soil in place, limiting erosion. Some trees, such as pines, make ground acidic.

▶ *Trees grow well in warm, damp climates.*

25

SOIL TAKES ITS TIME

New soil is made every day. It takes thousands of years of decomposition, weathering, erosion, and deposition to make soil fertile.

GROWING UP, GROWING DOWN

As the **parent rock** underneath breaks down, soil grows deeper into the ground. As new organic matter falls on top, the soil grows up. This process creates layers in the soil. In general, the older the soil, the thicker the layers become and the more fertile the topsoil.

LOOKING AT LAYERS

When you look at the ground, you see topsoil, full of dead plants and animals. Dig down and you find a layer full of minerals that have leached out of the topsoil. Even deeper you find rocky soil that has more recently broken off the parent rock. Finally, you get to **bedrock**, the underlying rock of the soil.

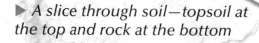

▶ *A slice through soil—topsoil at the top and rock at the bottom*

GONE IN AN INSTANT

Depending on the climate, it may take about 10,000 years to build **mature** soil. Unfortunately, soil can be destroyed much more quickly. When people remove plants, they expose sensitive soil to the harsh forces of our planet. Water, wind, and weather can attack the ground, leaving it lifeless.

▼ Topsoil has been washed away from this tree's roots.

◄ A tree slowly rots away in a rain forest, providing nutrients for a new tree to use and grow.

SOIL CONSERVATION

Most of us never think about soil. We take it for granted, but without it our planet would be very different.

▲ *A young fox stands at the entrance to its underground den.*

SAVING WILDLIFE

Imagine if there were no soil for a fox to make its home in, for worms to eat, or for birds to find worms in. Soil supports many food chains. These start with micro life, such as bacteria and fungi, include all plants, and end with plant- and meat-eating animals.

THIRSTY?

Soil provides clean water. As water soaks through the soil, it is cleaned. This action is a natural filtration system that people take advantage of.

NAKED AND STARVING

Just about everything we have and eat comes from the soil. Think about it: Without fertile soil, you would have no cotton jeans or T-shirts, no apples to eat, and no solid ground for your home. That is why soil must be conserved, or looked after.

▶ *If you look after soil, plant seeds in it, and care for the plants, you can grow lots of your own fruits and vegetables.*

YOU DIG IT

You can add nutrients to the soil by composting your fruit and vegetable scraps. To stop erosion, you can plant trees on hillsides and only walk on established paths. Most importantly, you can teach others what is special about soil.

▲ A lot of land is lost every year under roads and houses. We must all think carefully about the way we use Earth and soil.

29

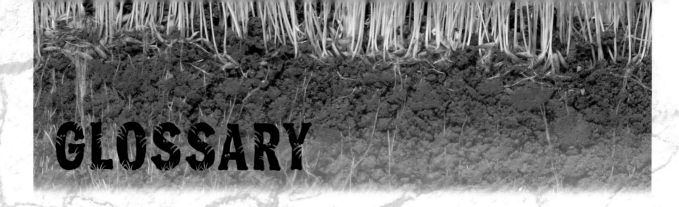

GLOSSARY

acidic A chemical that is sour like vinegar

aeration Making air spaces in the soil

basic A chemical that is bitter, such as soap

bedrock A layer of rock under the soil

compaction When soil is pressed tightly

decomposers Living things that break down matter into smaller parts

dissolve To break up in and become part of a liquid

enzymes Chemicals that cause a change in matter

erosion The process of being carryied away by water, wind, or ice

fertile To support plant growth

glacier A giant mass of ice that slowly moves downhill. It weathers and erodes rock

humus The organic material of soil

leach To dissolve out with water

legumes Plants that can change the form of nitrogen

lichen An alga and fungus that live together as if they were one organism

mature Fully grown

microbes Tiny living things such as some fungi and bacteria

mineral A natural solid substance that has never been alive

organic Living or once-living material

parent rock The lowest layer of soil made of solid rock

photosynthesis The way that plants make food from water and oxygen using sunlight as energy

pores Small spaces

sediment Small pieces of rock

silty Full of soil particles that are between the sizes of clay and sand

topsoil The upper layer of soil that is rich in nutrients

tundra A flat, cold area with very few trees

weathering The process of breaking down rock into smaller pieces

MORE INFORMATION

FURTHER READING

Down To Earth (Investigate Science). Melissa Stewart and Jeffrey Scherer. Compass Point Books, 2004.

Sand And Soil: Earth's Building Blocks (Rocks, Minerals, and Resources). Beth Gurney. Crabtree Publishing Company, 2004.

Soil! Get the Inside Scoop. David Lindbo and Others. American Society of Agronomy, 2008.

Soil. Rebecca Faulkner. Heinemann Raintree, 2008.

WEB SITES

Ask The Answer Worm, Natural Resources Conservation Service
www.nrcs.usda.gov/FEATURE/education/squirm/skworm.html
Dig It! The Secrets of Soil, Smithsonian Museum of Natural History
http://forces.si.edu/soils/index.html
Microbe Zoo: Dirtland, Digital Learning Center for Microbial Ecology
http://commtechlab.msu.edu/sites/dlc-me/zoo/zdmain.html
Rader's Geography4Kids!
www.geography4kids.com/files/land_soil.html

INDEX